LIFESCAPES

A Poetic Perusal of Life's Adventures

JON JACOBS

Cover: Photo courtesy of David Adam Beloff, Photographer
www.dabphotos.com

First printing 2011

ATTENTION CORPORATIONS, UNIVERSITIES, COLLEGES, AND PROFESSIONAL ORGANIZATIONS: Quantity discounts are available on bulk purchases of this book for educational, gift purposes, or as premiums for increasing magazine subscriptions or renewals. Special books or book excerpts can also be created to fit specific needs. For information, please contact:

Jon Jacobs, 233 Marsh Oaks Dr., Charleston, SC 29407
Ph. 843-478-9555
johnkul007@yahoo.com

PREFACE

This collection of poems represents a life-adventure. Many may tell your own story. Take time to peruse and meditate, but simply enjoy your experience and thoughts.

Dr. Jon Jacobs, born in Biloxi, Mississippi, into an Air Force family, has lived in Germany, France, and thirteen states. Poetry is an outlet for his adventures and relationships. A cousin of Edgar Allen Poe, Jon began his poetic writing at eighteen. 30 years a general and vascular surgeon, he now has a cosmetic and surgical dermatology practice.

After thirteen years of battling and winning his fight with lymphoma, he still composes poetry.

DEDICATION

To Him who is the past, the present, the ultimate future, our
Ground of All Being

To my parents, watching over me now

To my brothers and sister who continue to give introspective
criticism and love

To my wife and children, who love me in spite of myself

To my mentor, Carol Furtwangler, President of the South Carolina Poetry
Society, my heartfelt gratitude.

To my friends, communal family, teachers, professors, who molded me,
I give my heart and my thanks.

PROLOGUE

Lifescapes is a tale of adventures passed along in poetry, the musical written expression of who we are, where we have been, and our longing for future journeys. In this tale you will see me. And yourself.

Lifescapes is related in five modes:
Musings - Affective situations
Love Sought - Searching for our "one"
Love Engaged - Living with our "Love"
Love Lost - Alas, she has gone
Idiosyncrasies - Events, catastrophes, our
deep selves examined, a laugh, and our "all"

TABLE OF CONTENTS

MUSINGS

CALCULATED COCKTAILS

Cocktail party cornered
Collar starched and stiff
Drink half-full in one hand
Abstinence belied midriff
Brown stains on his teeth and nails
Sweat pouring from his brow
Surrounded by the products
Of success from past and now.
The nut bowl's long been emptied
French dip on his tie
Beyond weak jokes and then some
With one last chuckled lie
Religion, political parties,
The secretary's style,
All points of conversation
Sprinkled with pensive guile
Gauged humphs, rakish guffaws
Sneers and snively hot-airs blow
We must be most agreeable,
The Boss is here, you know.
Stale, gray cloud, familiar thick
The air hung just waist-high
Room-sized miniature of Downtown
A 5 o'clock rush-hour sky;

Another aimless cocktail fest
With just the town's invited best
Only the names change...
The faces are the same.

THAT OLD COAT

I've seen it worn so many times
A hand-me-down from old friends
Where have they gone?
So fashionable the pattern
When it was brand spankin' new
A flare, the cut, herring weave, too
The hint of sexy and dashing dare.

That old coat...
Less fashionable now
But functional, and "proper"
Befits the airs of the civic-minded
Career-focused, briefcase-swinging
Yes, practical, economical it is.

That old coat...
Comfortable, a little threadbare
But oh, so warm
Huddled on a bench
Beside longtime friends
Discussing politics
And the kids these days
Watching as the leaves fall
Our stone bench an island.

Those were the days
Money, sex, and power
The coat's kept me well,
Dressed for all occasions
Now it just touches other old coats
Shoulder to shoulder
And winks at winter coming
Once again.

RAMBLING

There was a time when I thought
I should never write to anyone
About my "peanut butter roses"
But would rather in my corner
Sit munching on them
While playing the "sole" "soul" man
On guitar
Drinking my half-empty
Never half-full
Cup of bitter black coffee.

It's sunny to have someone
To smell with you
The peanut butter of life
I only wish I could write in 3-D.
Even that hasn't enough depth.
Flat paper absorbs my ink-self
Flowing into the cellulose
Almost never fully extracted
By other eyes
With ink-absorbent retinas.

But smell the two-dimensional flower:
I want to look down
Omnipotently on the world.
The closest I ever was,
Standing on a mountain
Surveying the towns below.
Hardly the same
Looking down, down, down.
How far does down go
Before it becomes up?
I guess it depends
On which way you are traveling.

COFFEEHOUSE

We sit in quiet wonderment
'Round square candlelit tables
Pondering the meaning
Of paradoxical fables
Wrought by understanders
Played upon guitar
Questioning, answering
Who and what we are
We come a little closer
Not so much, but some
Ferreting out life-truths
Then half the battle's won.
Half the war is fought
Half the battle played
Just half the people realize
Our lives are but half-made
    To search
    To ponder
    To answer
    And then
    To question...

WEAVE

I examined it so very closely
Through fine thick ancient loupes
And followed each separate thread
The cottons, wools, and jupes
As they wound their way in concert
Each bound to pre-set paths
I watched them as they rose and fell—
Patterned corrugated laths.
They bore unique color splendid
Here white, there red and a navy blue
The sunlight bounced right off them
Riders giving each beam a hue.

Then I fell back a step or two
That I might not be remiss,
Envisioned the total masterpiece
A smile, a tear, a kiss...
The red was from a woman's purse
Clutched tightly to her breast—
Love's gift to her on taking leave
As war's unwelcome guest.
A spot of blue, so navy deep
From the corner of my eye
I saw was torn from old blue jeans,
Clad the saddened son nearby.
The white that piqued my every sense
Dazzling my mind anew
I saw on every villager
Crowding round the bier to view.

He was a part of each of them,
Their future, present, past;
He had helped raise every one
Their priest gone home at last.

6

As he lay quiet in coffin closed
Beneath the quilted flag
That they had made from what they had
Be it purse, or jeans, or rag,
The colors brilliant in the sun
Glistened boldly, wet with tears
Which prismed like a million stars
Branding memories for lifelong years.

MAKING MUSIC

All the poetry I could write in this life
Would only be an expression of who I am.
What thoughts play your heart chords?
What feelings resonate the strings of your life's orchestra?
What tunes do you play?
What arias bring you joy and what sonatas grief?
How can I ever plumb the depths of these?
Would you play them for me?
I want to know who you are, how you feel, what you feel.
How can I?
You always carry yourself so assuredly.
Low self-esteem you claim.
I don't see it.
You are the music
Full and complete.

<u>TIME</u>

Time is so ungrateful in its insistence.
We haven't much of it.
How can we protect ourselves
From its relentless chase?
We can, you know.
Time reminds me of a muscular dog.
You walk it or it drags you.
One must master.
How can I master time?
Ride it like a bull in a rodeo,
While it wears my body parts out?
In the end both win.
Time claims me.
As I reflect on the ride
I can see how I have won the contest.
The prize is mine as long as I stay on the bull
  To direct it.
  To control it.
  To master it.
How do you direct time?
Tell me of your rodeo struggles.
Where are you going?

<u>LOOKING BACK</u> (a grandson's thoughts)

I remember when I was little
And my eyes were round and blue.
My smile was infectious
And my admirers always coughed up laughs.
I would reach my tiny hand out to you,
Covered with applesauce and peas
You always took it and gently wiped it clean
Then touched it to your face.
My blond, silky hair was softer than the cat
And it got far more attention.
I remember the first word I said
And the look on your face
And the wet stuff on your cheeks,
Lifted high in a smile.
I think I cried once in a while
But new diapers made me stop.
One day I put my hand in my mouth
And there were two new white things
That were sharp.
I had to be very careful.
The plastic jug with the white stuff
And the soft floppy brown thing I sucked wasn't bad
But I missed your softness and being close.
We all have to grow up, don't we?
Yes, I miss the good old times,
But I have a lot to look forward to.
Now I am all grown up.
Now I am ONE!

Thoughts of my grandson to his Papa

RAINFALL

Torrential rain shouts at me
From my windshield
Deafening, blinding
Awash after thirty miles of free fall
Suicidal to final impact
Now lying in limp puddles
Reflecting dark clouds above
Glistening brightly jagged bolts
Deaf to their resounding voices
Ready for rolling, round rubber
As final dissipation.

Flowers open their mouths
Drinking wetness
Perspiring fragrance
Smiling in color
Swaying under pelting massage
Calling dinner to butterflies
Dreaming of the gentle teen
They will adorn as bold corsage.
Rainfall.
Life again eternal.
Called by the sun
For another journey.

FORTY YEARS

Forty thieves have stolen one year at a time
And you have found their treasure...
In a cave
At the bottom of your mind
Memories piled high
Stacks of vignettes,
Glimpses of friends' faces
As they changed over the decades
Of seasons never repeated,
But remembered and re-enjoyed...
The excitement, joy, fear and trepidation
Of the one bursting into your life
Changing it forever.
But in that cave there is a wee light
On the far side
You realize it is the exit
And the entrance of that cave
Which will remain a haven
To visit from time to time.
Through that tunnel you can see
The other side of the mountain,
Brilliant, sunlit and expectant—
The next Forty Years...

ANARCHY OF THE HEART

How long did senseless reign
Of feeling rule the heart?
Where all actions purposed
Deep within they start
Up from the center ushered
Protocol to write
To copy out in longhand
Dictums penned in spite
For no discerning cause
Reason then had fled
Data, schedules, certainty
Spewed forth, wasted, bled
As smiles of meaning crept then
When dawning thought birthed slow
Flew right in releasing
Kilowatts aglow
So what's the better way now?
Is it copy, hard and fast?
Or by our sight and sound selves
Governed, decided, cast
Moving towards our eighty years
Paragraphed by rest stops
Taking in the scenery
Chuckled forbearance adopts
Chaos gone awry now
To order given way
Once anarchy of the heart
In peace holds fact at bay,

MEMORIES BECOME US

They waft like picturesque leaves
All about in another time and place
Memories were floating from ages past
And those not yet formed
While I was stitched together in the womb
Familiar and not
They came into the birthing room
Landing on the sticky poster board,
A living collage, my story
With a simple word at the bottom,
My name.

The genes I wear, so comfortable, warm
What color are chromosomes,
What is their scent?
No matter
They are where I have been,
Desire to go, to walk or run,
To lean or stand or cry
To grasp at minutes pushing by.

LOVE SOUGHT

BOTTLED LOVE

A crystal bottle of green love
Lay docile on my dresser
While shafts of languid light
Pushed through its smoky sides.
It must have thought, as bottles think
That days are given solely to drink
Nostalgic moments
In sips of impassioned memories.
It never travels far
This timeless, dust-covered jar,
Ne'er far save in spirited light-years
Voyaged with past lovers' eyes and ears
Hearts endeared and lives enshrined
In lead glass, clear as now
Opalescent past, and future, too.
But you, you the clarity constrained
Until one day it dropped and drained.
The decanter slowly emptied,
Its bright green gave way
To sweet air clear
The jar still sits, quite happily, queer
Like a Mona Lisa smile it winks
Pondering your wonderment.

AN EVENING OF FRENCH

Rivulets of conversation
Drip like honey from your smile
Splashing on my cheeses and French croutons
Washed down with vintage wine
Return to you with bright blue eyes
Reflected in your chocolate browns
Dancing with schoolgirl delight.
Our talk meanders along seamless miles,
Unexplored and ancient paths,
Some by chance, some carefully chosen
A Lewis and Clark expedition
To discover new territories
Rummaging through Paleolithic ruins
Of stale relationships
With each rise and fall of hope
Presenting a new horizon desperate for congruity
Yet comfortable in an unspoken commonality
What did she say?
What has he meant?
He is so old…
She is so young…
There is the plank we walk
To the delight of alligators
And pirates of our destiny
We move step by step
Blindfolded with senses keen
Expectant that this last plunge
Will deliver us into that eternal hope
Enveloping us like an azure Caribbean sea
In that we drown, laughing silently
Sealed with a final interrogatory,
A temple kiss.

FAIR LADY

Fair lady of heart's summer drought
Who slakes my thirst like Spring rain
Soft and delicate her fabric,
Her covering lines every gentle contour—
Her skin catching evening's sun, turning hues
Prism-like into a palette of pastels—
Few sights have drawn such yearning...
Few moments given such pull—
To simply reach and touch such rich and velvet skin—
Just to touch and nothing more.
Such gentle face and laughing lines,
Parenthesized by dimples,
Calls forth my own joyful laugh in response.
If I had her for one starry night, all to myself—
What a wonder to see those tiny sequins,
Canopied light, sprinkle light shafts
Down on her golden hair—
It would only take one such breathless moment to assure me
I would lack nothing by spending the rest of my time
Just so--a captive of that very time capsule.
You are the stuff from which dreams are made—
It is you...yes, it is you...it is you.
If she would turn to me and look
For one brief moment, I think I would melt,
And if not I would remain some clear substance
For her to grab and hold.
At once she can see clear through me—
Would that it be for who I want to be
And not who I am...

GOLDEN GIRL

In Days of Dreams and Fantasies
When Balmy Spring blows through
I cast my thoughts out to the wind
That bears them searching you.
Finding yours they light caress
Brush fingers through your hair
Then crawl neatly beside your mind
To feel the way you care.

They seek you out long weeks gone by
Straining each silent hour
Listening for the sibilant chords
That mark your song's strange power
The arias playing cacophony
Waft to melody
Your azure eyes discovered here
Beam forth your symphony.

The vision of that Golden One
Danced and laughed, then knew
My simple mind laid bare before her
Exposed, naked, true.
She intuited, saw in the lair
Hiding ecstasies long buried
Her searching eyes peered past my shell,
My patchwork world she queried.

Viewed it through windows of my eyes,
Gazed beyond my soul,
Flickering light burned brightly still
My love, my life, my whole—
She reached out her hand to touch
Wresting him from the night
He reposed 'longside at last
Nestled next down-soft delight

Quelling endless void within,
Warmth and depth swept clear
Present Vision real arms held,
Gently drew him near
Her sweet scent swirled full around him
Drugging him with her smell
He now knew he couldn't loose her
Turn, turn, life's carrousel!

HEART STRINGS

I have a problem.
I've got hold of someone's heartstrings.
It's not a very big string
Just a small strand.
I'm holding on for all it's worth.
It's a silver strand.
If I don't pull at all,
The heart turns in other directions
Looks away, daydreaming
Forgetting about this hand
Holding the string.
Pulling too often
Irritates the delicate heart,
Makes it terribly uncomfortable
I've tried pushing the string.
You simply can't push a string
And make any effective headway
So I end up pulling on it
Trying to pull ever so gently
Too hard, it will rip right out of the heart
Too lightly, I sit holding a handful
Of beautiful string
But I can't quite make heads or tails
Of what I should do with it.
Heartstrings are delicate things, you know…

SILENCE

Whispers in breathless air
To a yearning ear
A heart that breathes its own pity
Beating not for itself
But for another
Who does not know its loneliness
Nor sees its loveliness
Hope is in the beating itself
That emanates the very life
Which drives it onward
Offering soft messages to its beloved
Yearning for them to be captured,
Enjoyed, understood, caressed, savored
Matrixed, enmeshed as a vine and lattice
That is who I am
No more
No less
But all that
For you.

SURREAL

More important than breath itself
Than life beating pulse
The gift of desire fulfilled
Chemistry that welds two
Their deepest separate passions
Weep without the other
A perfectly shaped void
Empty, longing is the sole soul
That would mold skin, heart, mind
In impassioned lifelong embrace
A restful completeness
That smiles tears to say
It is you that I breathe
That pulses within me
Now I sleep and awake
In surreal life
Without beginning,
Without end,
Our Mandela eternal.

PIANO TRIPLET

Like a triplet on a piano
Words roll off your tongue,
Soft, light and sensual,
The penetrating rhythm
Of "I love you".
Behind follows the swell,
The emotional exclamation point,
The heart-throb of joy,
Tagging along like a wagging puppy's tail.

I bask in the summer's warmth
Of your speech and your soul.
It wipes against my face,
A velvet glove
Urging me to envelope you
As a delicate breeze.
To touch, to caress the Who that you are,
Tickle your skin, bristle its hairs,
Return the scintillating sensations
You offer me so freely.

Yes, a piano triplet
Echoes the "I love you".

LOVE ENGAGED

DREAMS

How sweet the dreams that dress the night
That fire one's heart with brief delight
Undispelled by morn's first light
And breathed throughout the day.

Sonnets poured from poet's tongue
Heart's miseries and joys are sung
On which his hopes and fears are hung
His soul bared on display.

And you, the Golden Haunt of dreams,
The Mystery lure of scented steams
Vapors formed to contoured schemes
Morosely held at bay.

How long before my self awakes...
An empty room, save bleared opaques
You, lost again as dream forsakes—
Carpe-Diem—Seize the Day!

LIGHTLY

Lightly did she stand before me
Lightly come, and lightly gone.
Her presence like a wisp of willow
A faint breeze brushing my mind
So fleeting I couldn't catch her
So pure I dared not touch her—
A scent and laughter,
Breath of gaiety, hinting jubilee
Summer's cloud given form
Only by thought caresses.
I yearned for her to stay.
Other places beckoned her.
She was lightly come, and lightly gone.
Here I wait on her tomorrow—

SKYLIGHT AFTERNOON

Voyeur beams of sun shafts
Through the skylight play,
Dance on heavenly bodies
Embellishing sensuous display
Of love, and rapture, of life-breathed clay
We are but dust, delicately ordered
Arranged in ethereal style
Lost in mutual wonderment
Each others' gaze beguile
Dreams of lovers all the while
With consensual inspirations
Of symphonic orchestration
Our movements flow as honey
Sweet and thick consecration
Filling voided years with our oblation.
We are but two in seas of destined pairs
Cast off by others who withdrew love's claims
Lonely, lovely, filled with gratuitous gifts,
Our Diogenes-search with separately guided aims
Divined us along parallel fames
Whose grandeurs are only seen through soul-mate eyes
To love, to hold, to please, to comfort, and to give
Today, and today, and today, as long as todays shall live...

CLOUDS

You are my cloud, and my ground
Your smell, your touch, your smile
The fervor, vim and vigor,
Energy anthropomorsed,
Vibrant in you as a woman
Exhilarant in emanating your love
I, as a solar sponge, absorbing your rays.
If you were a nuclear power plant,
The whole universe could shine for a millennium
From your wondrous lustrous splay.

I am so happy that you are so happy...
It is what I strive for, live for
To make you smile
Make you laugh
Make you live,
To do it all beside you.

Breakfast with you in your robe
Would be a pleasure
Too rapturous to even dream.
I love you in your robe.
You are so sensuous.
I love to come up behind you and caress you,
To kiss your neck, to hug your body,
Watch you cooking while I am steaming.

Know this,
When there is a moment,
A remote minute instance,
I will be with you.
When I am not there to caress you,
I will be beside you, dreaming I am with you.
I love you
Forever.

BEACH GETAWAY

Sunshine drew tall shadows on undulant sand
I was taller than you
You giggled louder
Our smiles raced each other to dimples
And both won
Looking at you horizontally
On a warm blanket
Under molten sunlight
Gave new perspective
To your loveliness
You showed me your hair
I caressed its softness
We both said "ouch"
As we rolled over the sand spurs
You purred
While I sighed
Holding you in my arms
Is completion of a completely beautiful day
The sound of your voice,
Of the waves,
Of my heartbeat,
Coalesce in wonderment
The wonderment of love.

GRASS

The slurry of green beneath my feet
That sneaks between my toes
The wrinkly carpet so fresh and clean
Its earthiness tweaking my nose
Stirs wintered hearts alive again
Peaks my interest in the Spring
Studded by charms of joyous jonquils
Patterning deft weaver's looming
Mayday chants its tunes anew
Carpeting nearby hills
Like a swelled sea which pitches and rolls
Over ridges and rills
The hues that tingle all my senses
In the distance coalesce,
Calm my waking soul once more
Feeling my heart effervesce
Rich spring grass in the countryside
Ballooning me up in the air—
Lifts me tall inches off the ground
Just to leave it lying there.

GREEN GRASS

I remember the green grass that year.
Ah, yes, the grass. Ahh, y e s –
That bountiful, luscious green grass powdering the hillock
That fell gently to the broad, quiet river below,
Breeze pushed its fingers gently though my hair,
Brushing my face with its tendrils.
The smell of lilacs dizzying my heady gaze
I contemplated a dog changing into a duck
In the clouds billowing above,
Carrying my thoughts with them.

Spring. Lusty spring.
She rolled over lithely beside me
Almost capsizing the cup of wine between us.
We both sipped and giggled,
Each holding the other in a spellbinding gaze,
A moment all too short.
Her long flowing light and flowery spring dress
Pulled demurely to her knees.
Contrasting pastel colors,
Breathtaking against her soft, blondest of blond skin.
And I told her so.
Her only response was a shake of her beautiful head of hair
Accentuated by a brilliant blush framing that delicate face.

Poison. Poison, I thought,
As I leaned towards the nape of her neck.
I loved that perfume.
Somehow I knew I would grow to love it more.
An afternoon filled with laughter, and Eros, and meaning—
How could she be so frank and transparent,
So fresh, simple, yet as complex as a Rubik's cube?
Her puzzle I would never solve, only enjoy.

You have to sneak up on a bird.
You have to stalk, and stalk, and...balk; and gawk!
And squawk, and...stalk.
Sooner or later – no, never.
I would fly with her, never capture her.
Beauty is flight's freedom,
Watching the carefree, thrilling flight
Of so predictably unpredictable a creature.

I could tell she didn't believe me.
No matter.
She enjoyed being with me,
Enjoyed the laughter, and the hugging,
Hushed moments of secret understanding,
My embarrassed honesty.
She enjoyed what I enjoyed.
I suppose the next step is trust.
Or abandonment. Or backgammon.
Maybe the next step is not to step but to crawl.
We have all the time in the world to crawl.

As long as one can admire and love,
One is young forever.
I lingered over her,
Watching her wave to the fishermen just off shore.
How I...
How I love green grass in the springtime.
I grabbed a handful and smelled its freshness.
She pulled a piece away,
Taught me how to make a whistle,
Blowing the blade between her thumbs.
How I love green grass—

EYES

Your eyes cannot your love disguise
Nor hands belie gentle moods
Your very breath in syncopated sighs
Moves in concert with heaving breast, exudes
Your very soul, peninsular and surrounded
With all the seas that mold your mortal being,
Shape the tenderness expounded
By your smile, your passion, your joy beyond all seeing.
Who shall receive this packet, rich and fair?
Would he be worthy of the golden balm
Extruding from every pore and without care
Heals those whose fortunes summon stroking palm
Inebriating senses long ago forgot
To pacify the ills that strangle future's calm?

DANCE WITH ME

Close you were,
And soft,
Real, so real
Your alluring green eyes,
Direct and penetrating...
I, captive of your enigmatic smile
Danced and danced again
To a song of past.
And future, too,
A song that we both knew
Not only by memory, but in our souls
As if we had moved in concert
Some Spring day in ages past
I could have held you long and long again
And never left the room
In my mind it is so...
In my dreams that won't let go
Sweet reveries linger on
Long past daybreak, into morn
Those dreams break out in dimples
On my face in unexpected moments
Walking down the halls
Or in conciliatory conversations
I know they wonder at my Cheshire Cat smile...
It is for you.

SHORT BUT SWEET

I bask in your love,
I kneel before your forgiveness
I stand face to face to the fullness of who you are
I weep at your sorrow
I long to be with you in your loneliness
I smile at the promise of tomorrow
I joy at the thought of our yesterdays
I would be one with you

BEACHCOMBER

You captivate me
Like the sound of the sea,
Engulf me
As the rolling waves
Fly high above me
Free as the seagulls
Lie beneath me
As my foundation,
The very sands of the earth.
You turned gently beside me
The heavy velour shirt and pants
Covering your softness
I crushed your contour with my fingertip…lightly
You dozed…I snuggled.
Sometime in the night
You got up and looked at the stars
I looked at you.
You dozed…I snuggled
Hours I lay next to you
Kissing lightly, stroking softly
You wiggled…I snuggled
I remember dawn creeping over the ocean
Seeing your beauty in the first light
Finally I rolled towards you
Burying my face on your neck
You rolled onto your back
I hovered over you like a summer fog.

RADAR LOVE

Does love have radar?
Does it fly "IFR"?
Can it weather storms?
How brief?
How fierce?
What about clouds that block its vision?
Or deepest night
Where even the strongest guiding beacon
Is smothered in blackness?
What about flying in ice-storms
When one lover is feeling a bit cool?
How about seeing ahead
Avoiding thunderstorms in its path?
As long as I have a small radio,
A means of communication,
I can fly in any kind of weather
  Anytime
    To any destination—
Talk to me
Tell me where you are...

LOVE LOST

ROSES

A thousand roses would I give you,
Buy the whole red fragrant field
In some fair glen
To seal your heart
Set it afire and amend
The hurts, the wounds
The tears I've served
Sweet melody, golden lass
Hues of cream and primrose mingled
Draped in ivory silk for skin
It is you I smell and feel
And talk to in my dreams
You I dance with my whole life through
Come dance with me...

YOUR NAME

The syllables of your name

Fall out onto my pillow

Like scrabble letters.

Forming them into utterance

Is completing.

They lie beside my smiles

And summon me.

GAZE

Could she have known?
It was in her eyes
And some brief moments
Years gone by
It flickers still...
That smile, innocent longing,
Distant, familiar gaze.

My deepest self knows
It will have been...
No, it was the world's greatest love story.
The story lingers
Between mid-waking twilight hours
When dreams are dreams
And substance, too.

My heart still aches
Peering through cobwebbed remembrance
Around corners too painful to turn,
Down sandy roads too pristine to mar
With my lone footsteps.
Little beads of sweat
Line up Indian-file
Along furrows of a once-youthful brow.

How I wish that we had coalesced,
Joining, drifting, following the lay of the land
Simply for togetherness
Not caring about final destination.
Whether by my selfishness,
Her trepidation,
Or another's scorn,
I will never know,
But suspect all three
Were the brick masons
Of the wall erected.

It was May.
Winter bleakness blown away,
Light breezes swelling the air,
Demure sweetness scenting flowered fields.
My soul became an unleashed falcon.
This time my gaze did not pass through her, beyond her.
She absorbed me completely.

MY PLEA

There was a time when through dark lanes I walked,
My great fear that shadows might snuff me out
Alone, inside, on my dusty road I stalked
I sought the truth that promised crucifixion of all doubt.

A poignant scene awoke me from my reverie with a jolt
Sweat dripping from my nightclothes like a river poured
Cold excitement as a bullet chambered by the bolt
The vision of my beloved woman my whole soul adored.

Long it was since we began our fiery fest
That brought to close all doubts, and longer still
Walked we hand in hand together in our quest
Absorbed in mind and heart which both our love did fill.

Days, weeks, months loved we with equal passioned breath,
Memories branded immortal in our hidden thought
Those were the days our very selves given up in death
Would be too small a token of our love paid thus and bought—

Now it seems our steamy course has slowed its pace
Our blood no longer rushes to inflame gentle body parts
Flush of anger more oft reddens fair complected face
Our heads contrive the words we exchange, not our hearts.

In your absence my very soul cries out, tears rage on.
I've squeezed the life from the one I've held as dear
An abyss of proportioned horror splits my self now you are gone
I lie hopeless, empty, besieged with all life's fear

If I could change the hated deeds that to you I've cruelly done,
Bring you back that we might finish life embraced
To any cost I would accomplish be it all I own
So small a price I offer you – heart's poverty abased.

WHAT IS NIGHT?

What is night that I should sleep,
Closing my eyes, and not see thee?
What is day that I should arise,
And not see thee with my eyes wide as owls'?
What is love, that I not take you in arms,
Breathe against thy breast?
Or should I, that I not breathe at all,
To feel your very soul close by?
What is life without thee
That I should do all things in solitude,
Would be existence only,
That desert spent,
A solitary star midst uncountable nebulae,
Cold, oh, so cold...
You are the sun that heats me,
The wind that cools me,
The water that washes me,
The wings that give me flight...

SIGHS

Leaden sighs sank to the valley floor
Shrouded by umbrage
In the canyons of sorrow.
There they heaved and breathed,
Listed, fell.
There they died
Alongside my friend
Crippled, beaten, soundless.

The plains, meadows, deep ravines,
Once cool with Spring laughter,
Were silent.
Deadly, and finally, silent.
Paralyzed by one fell blow
Transecting the center
Of his very being.

He lay completely, utterly, still
Not a cell respired.
Cattle-like people herds
Would wander and trample him
With their prattle,
Berate him with conjectures,
Moisten him with dung
Of accusation.

All this would not be so terrible
Were his thoughts not also blinded
In this abject poverty of love,
Of connection with even one other soul.
What is greater hell
Than isolation from lifelong friendships,
Than the journey
From shore, to peninsula, to island?

There is none.
There is none to greet you.
There is none to share your bread.
There is none to share your bed.
There is none.

Breathe on.
Breathe on.
In the uttermost darkness
Is there not a single photon of caring?
A tiny packet of loving?
If so, let me see it now.
Let me feel it.
Let me sense its warmth.
Be here in my night.
Be there in my morrow.

GHOST

I am in love
With the ghost of who we were,
With the firmament
Of who we shall be
The latter more precious than the former
We shall shine like gold and burn like fire.
Few will ever conceive our nadirs,
Nor attain those zeniths,
Take a breath as a single being,
Move in concert as one symphony
But that shall be
You and me.

MY LOVE

Love lay beside me
Impressioned on her pillow
Familiar sweet fragrances
Spiraling heavenward,
Scented candle-smoke.
I grope for her, blind
Staring through opaque saline
Falling to round, wet ponds
On well-worn satin sheets.
My tongue turns her name
Holding, caressing it
Then allowing it to spill out
Among other words of pleading apology
But she has fled this taciturn life
Not unscathed, for my grasping marks
Are not hidden by her wry smile.
My love was embodied power
Holding her slave, and I, the master
I, shackled all the more by her embrace
Comforted under her yoke
Now lonely and frightened by freedom.

RETROSPECT

Tears cannot answer in the wake of Winter's loom
Weaving its alabaster tapestry
Reflecting clean the void of heart's lost ebony rose,
My soul's delight for lo these many years
Gone, gone to freedom's fields
Far more vast than any ocean's frothy tides,
Far more peaceful than wretched verbose wisdom
Or stolen sunsets, however bronzed with sweet asides.

She wandered, nay, ran, from raving grasps,
From lies, yea, barren deceits
Disguised as exquisitely sculpted ice.
That she left was fortune spun to gold for her
But fathomless Hell of loneliness
For the bastard son of all ill.

Will life play this violin,
Unfinished concerto laid in present minor mode?
Without voice, without melody,
Beating harsh rhythm in each lonely heart.
Will it end in descant
Never striking more melodious chords,
Are there after-rest sonatas to be sung?
Life itself will be so incomplete
Dearth of borrowed time
Against which to compete
For all affections.

At night I lie and wrestle horrific dreams,
Mocking visions of how we used to be
Begging for dawn to dispel night's coldest bonds.
When it comes, I pine away the day,
Marveling at the slowness of the creeping hours
Wasting into sleepless evening once again.

I am but a shallow breath away from ceasing.
One day you will look my way
But it will then be too late.
Your gaze will be upon a mere shadow of who I was
That glance shimmered by a single tear...

We'll be gone, you and I
Sailing some distant sea
Perhaps with partners, though foreign they will be
Never will we draw comfort from another
As had we once together, ethereal and free.

Perhaps that is our allotted verdict
Then again, maybe not
We have our choices in the lot
Long as our hearts remain unbound
We can unearth the lost, and when found
Rekindle sacred fires long extinguished
To blaze and warm,
To light our way once more
That we might seal our very souls,
A bond that breathes on, and on

Reach back and forward
Stretch with all your might
Touch my face and beckon me to come
To form an unbreaking circle
Infinite infinity and beyond
Reach, reach through the pain and tears
Through the deadness and the fears,
Reach just once more,
I'll be there.

LOVE WARRIORS

Showers of promises
From teasing, rainless clouds
Trickle tears from lonely loving eyes
Till long last glint
Of rainbow light
Glanced off a sharpened scimitar
Love-wielded
Proffered once more's hope
In hearts à deux,
Warring Beastie's head of hate
Falls at their feet
Now they stand tall and twined
For long and long to come.

A DAY WITHOUT HER

A day without her is an eclipse
Shrouded umbrance without sunshine
A parched journey
Into desert wasteland
Seeing as a colorblind man
Watching the brilliance of a rainbow
Perceiving only variegations of brown
It is to travel under clouds
To feel cold rain on dry skin,
Shiver without arms to warm and caress,
To long without fulfillment
A gnawing emptiness etching a clay heart
Is a journey into unknowing
Without hope for the future
Reminded only of past's bliss
It is unbearable
It is unrequited love
I love her as an eternal soul mate
None other can take her place
None other ever will.

SIXTY YEARS

Where have they gone
Where will they flow
Those fluid memories
Acid moments
Sweet tea kisses
Pulsing heartaches
Soft-skinned blisses
Starlit studded evensongs
Lingering till rosy dawns
Awakening alongside you
Breathtaking reminiscence,
Two that were one
How long?
How long has it been
How long will it be
For us together
And separate, we?
Ages gone and eons come
Sixty years is all I ask
When they are full spent
We'll look back
To breathe the scent
Of love once shared
Or bound as one
And know our lives
Were both best done
Apart -
And together

IDIOSYNCRASIES

SEPTEMBER 11TH

September 11, the radical operation
On a country infected by a silent disease
The scalpel that carved out a cancer:
The indifference of our souls

Smoke billowed heavenward,
Prayers crying for comfort
For answers to why
From the towers pierced
By our own supreme technology.

Blind cataracts of our mundane milieu
Crumbled in those early hours.
Days we cried for reasons
Of unanswerable horrors
Inflicted by an entity yet unknown

Who is my brother?
He who raced into the buildings
He who sifted through the ashes
Weeping for those he never knew
The brave who stood up to terror in the sky
Men, women, who now stand vigilant as protectors

Amber waves of grain,
Her purple mountains
A nation grounded on God's love
America gathers a people once again
United in bonded brotherhood
We will ever stand firm.

HURRICANE HUGO

The winds blew…
I saw them all around,
Felt them tear at the soul of the land
Ancient sentries snapped, and snapped again
The trees bowing down before its fury
Not in worship but in submission
Their exalted years surrendering
Mustering not even a silent curse
Something left with the winds
Stripping all creatures from the countryside
In awe exhausted men gaped.
Empty, desolate, wasted
"It was like a war zone"
Though few had seen a battle
The ache was for a loved one lost
Torrents of rain and tears
Blurred visions
Blinded by cataracts of memories destroyed
Strewn as seaweed along endless beaches
Old photographs, bits of others' lives
Knew no boundaries or surveyors' markers
Like stray dogs they had wandered aimlessly
Deposited as evidence of unforgettable ravage
Now is the hour
Birth and death lie separated
By a narrow ravine of time
Over which we may jump
Or crawl
Or glide.
By wings eternal
I will glide.

LOST GEM

New or old the twain shall meet
Broken levee flows defeat
Post tortuous winds
Once whistling soft down streets aglow
With shouts aloft midst arias of saxophones
Cheered by frozen Hurricanes tendering memories
Of not so long ago
Dreams float away
On rafts of visions grown cold
Beaded rowdy Mardi Gras
Parading crowded Bourbon Street
Fat Tuesday now turned lean
How many lovers gazed
Across beignets at Café du Monde
Lips wet with sips of chocolate java
Sucking in the Cajun and Bananas Foster
Thank you New Orleans
Our souls cry for those
Who are no more
For the legacy burned indelibly
Revisited only in quiet respite
A gem now stolen
But precious through all ages.

COLLEGE MEMORIES

Exam week studies
Western Civilization slammed shut
An hour to think glorious thoughts
Remembering the girl
With the red hair and dimpled smile
A smile that if you trip
You can fall into ever so deeply
A mind stretched so far
That even the stars cannot be contained.
The same girl that found you
Lost on a warm summer's day
Sprinkled with butterflies and jumping fishes
Running along white sanded beaches.
Those were the days.

Living in the future, reminiscing the past
But never living now for the now
For now alone is not now together
Bearable existence against beautiful living
Existing for "Hello, quietly"-brought silences
Stuffed with cream filling of knowing
And while knowing
Silence screams meaning softly,
Whispers to the mind - all.

Shell enclosing, encasing
As memory fades
Reality laughing from all four walls
Cracked paint sadistically smiles,
Grim façade teaching me façading
A veneer, not sheer, sneers and jeers
And tears hear, and sear
The mere peer, so dear, so near
Clear, year after year, then veers
No longer to appear, only to fear...

Thus ends the ending
And nothingness to begin
Only to start-
As thin as life, a heartbeat
A mind polluted with "thinks"
As an ocean salt-saturated
Carries me further...forever
For within without
Reality calls - screams -
Battering paper-mâché memories
And lifelong philosophies
Which must push from the inside
To keep the outside
From crushing me.

EXAM SANCTUARY

The green plaster hermitage lulls,
The student attempted crawling
Backward into dreams of reality
Long ago awaits
Away from rhetoric
And matters that don't
To realness left behind.

A flit of candle whips
Sparkled blaze sears
A charcoal design of joy
Exposed a sunshine moment
Unenshrouded by umbrage
Tastes of the wind brushing tongue

Unleashed, the joy explodes
Wheeling, reeling, glancing cloud-ward
Shouts, screams!
A nod, cracking head solidly on the typewriter
Another bit of plaster falls
From the walls...
Then began the silent memories
Pressing behind burning eyelids

A race along the sands
Spray of tiny droplets
Cools our steaming bodies.
Freedom bursts forth
Gently touching palms
Of the other half of my love

Verdant shell of hermitage
Alive with years of past,
Never letting it seep through
To the outer, to them
Plastered on plaster walls
And the plaster...falls

ASHES

Now another torture,
Greater than the first...
Will ashes burn??
I see my pile, neatly swept
In the center of an empty bedroom floor,
Surrounded by so much space.
A summer breeze sneaks under the door
Lapping at the edges of the grey heap.
Some fragile flakes flutter upward,
The remains shudder a collective sigh,
Too deep for words,
Too dry for tears,
Too quiet for almost any sound at all,
Sit lightly and heavily on the cold wood.
I remember when the ashes had substance,
Movement and life, smiles and laughter,
All manner of good will.
Yes, I remember.
Do those sparkling green eyes
Still behold this mound of disarticulate mud?
The lips are both wondrous and dangerous.
Wondrous at the velvet caresses on my former self,
Dangerous that they hold the very breath
That can blow these ashes
Into a cloud of dismembered passions.
I cringe.
I am waiting...for a kiss...or an exhalation
I cringe
And hope.

LIFE OF A LEAF

And the leaf drifted down,
  Separated from the tree
And the leaf floated,
  Following behind the man
And the leaf was muddied
  By a truck
And the leaf was dashed
  Against the steps
And the leaf looked up
  At the man and wondered
"And the man doesn't fall,
  Or trip, or be thrown about?"
And then another man
  Crushed the leaf with his step
And the first man looked pitifully
  At the leaf
And to himself said
  "Man's life is like a leaf"
And the leaf was swept aside
  And the leaf rotted.

FOOL

What is a fool?.
I am a fool.
Can a fool recognize himself,
Or must others always point it out?
Does the realization come suddenly
Like an explosion in a tomato factory
Covering him with malodorous red rottenness?
Does it creep on like algae in a stagnant pond?
Can a fool feel?
Can a fool fool?
How long does a fool live?
For himself? For others?
How do you discard a fool,
Rid yourself of the malignant little bother?
A little enticement and he lingers by,
Like the unpleasant smell of old English Leather
Too copiously applied.
He'll die of dehydration—
Millions of silent tears—
How do you know a fool?
Ask one.
Ask me. I know.
I am a fool.

STONE MAN

That onetime heart of clay
Molded to everyman's whim,
Brought sunshine forth as day
Contoured by reverent verses of their hymn
Reaching deep to others' inner selves...
The smiles that leapt forth
When he spoke and queried
Just how are you—really?
Is your sorrow truly buried?
The Empathetic Soul
Stretched out like centipede runners
Searching, always searching
The life-giving water of another's hurts.
Meeting the red of anger
And the blue of tears
With painted desert colors of sensitivity.

Years have worn him down.
Desiccated souls insidiously sipping
Until the clay heart began to dry and dry.
First it was the humor that left.
Then the happy lines about the eyes.
Tired - oh, how tired - or was it ennui?
Finally someone stopped long enough
To knock on his heart...
It knocked back - the deadened sound,
Soft, yet deafening - of stone.
That passerby jettisoned the stony heart
Like a shot-put.

It rolled and came to rest
In a shallow wet puddle of someone's tears.
It sponged the wetness dry—
So thirsty for all we thirst for—
Then softened - just a bit - enough to notice.
To notice itself
To notice those tears disappeared.
A smile crept on like dawn
Pushing shadows away in the early morn.
Time again, and another time.

REALITY

Just where does it begin, and where end
This stuff of reality?
The forward part of my mind says now is here,
Surrounding time of before and after never were,
Then never will be—
 I know it is not so.
The backward portion sees
The past as through smoked glass,
Weeding out rotten-apple memories
Planting carnations and violets
In fields of forgotten vignettes,
Special moments longed for—
Mind's eye lanes less traveled,
Lacing lost love forests...
Or perhaps not lost,
Just laid aside, a bit overgrown
Forever watered by the babbling brooks,
Bitter-sweet passions meandering by.
Follow it–follow it past the now
Into the year's end hopes—
The goal so highly sought,
The wandering, the journey,
This is the now.
The reality I've looked so long for.
I glance here and over there, all about,
For someone's hand to pull, to push, to hold.
Someone's.
Whose?

BREAKIN' OUT

It started out as a good day,
A Friday I believe it was.
It was just another weekend
To "billow our sails" as it oft does.
Then came along this "Jesus" thing
I gathered from flappin' jaws
He was "just another madman,
Dyin' for a silly cause."

Another band of followers,
Scraggly, poor, misguided and blind
You'd think they'd see clear through him,
His scheme and purpose behind
All his syrupy kindness,
The miracles and stuff-
But as the floggings weakened him
You could see he wasn't that tough.

Although it was somewhat curious
The manner this person held
After being beat and spat upon
His fiery eyes "Love" spelled.
For many stood by watching-
I felt sorry for the chap
Especially when they donned him
With the robe and thorny cap.

I remember quite clearly
My own mouth parched and dried.
The thirst I knew was his,
Dragging the tree undignified.
Thank goodness for those women
Weeping loudly there close by.
They at least had a chance to help him
And wiped his sweat-face dry.

There was another Godsend,
Simon, I think his name ran;
A passer-by, pressed into service.
What an ill-chosen man.
Then I've often pondered
That there may have been a "glue,"
A mysterious force of love, or such,
That welded the hearts of the two

There we were, trudging along now,
Up to the hill of the Skull.
We all knew what was at the top-
In the mayhem there was a slight lull.
I heard one stander-by's deep gasp
As they laid him on the tree–
"Why are they nailing him alone?
Why not just tie all three?"

The soldiers pounded those fat wrist nails.
It was apparent they must be assured
That this Jesus whom they crucified
For all time would be secured.
When I saw this innocent young man
My heart began to boil
As they lifted him high in agony,
My mind in fierce turmoil!

Just for a split second there
I saw him looking at me
Out of the crowds around us
Into MY heart he could see.
Open the window of your soul,
Close your eyes for a moment or two.
See those pained, kind eyes of Jesus
Looking you through and through.

"I never did great wrongs, dear Sir"
"Yes, but you're far from me–
Come closer, I'll give you joy and peace
And set your bound heart free."
Right then my palms began to sweat
I could see that he was right.
Where was the joy, the peace, the hope
I'd fought for with all my might?

His searching gaze as I beheld
Said plain enough to me
"Come closer, I've done all the work
Give me YOU, and I'll set you free."
That's what I did midst the bustling noise,
As I saw him drinking the gall.
"Take my angry, selfish 'me'–
Just as I am" - and He took it all.

I hung around till just before three,
The crowds had all gone but a few.
A storm was blackening the skies.
A threatening uneasiness grew.
For the first time in a while He spoke-
"Forgive them. They know not what they do"
As in a cry of deep anguish
He began shouting Psalm Twenty-Two.

He looked at his mother
And a man named John,
And afterwards gazed at me.
"It is finished," He gasped in his final breath
But I knew that's not all there'd be.

The lightning, the clouds and the furious rain,
The ground shaking under my feet,
Are all but a lost, fading memory
As I went over to take my seat
Beside John and His mother Mary,
Where we sat for the rest of the day,
Crying, sobbing and searching
For words—but there was nothing to say.

I helped them take Him down from the cross
Carrying him to the tomb.
We heaved and shoved this huge round rock
To seal off that precious room
Where all my life's past doubts were laid,
And all my future's dreams,
For I had given away my heart...
My loves, my worries, and schemes.

I knew that something more must come,
Just what I couldn't tell.
All Saturday we moped around
And, I'm sure felt a taste of Hell.
The doubts, the fears and loneliness
Threatened to choke our light.
Where would we go, what would we do?
"Father, hear us in our plight!"

That night's sleep was a fitful one,
Must have waked a dozen times.
But finally came the Sunday dawn
Roused by the temple chimes.
As I got dressed and ready to go
There was a frantic knock at the door.
Mary, hysterically happy with joy,
Cried, "Jesus' body—it is no more!"

It was hard to make sense of her scattered words.
Thank goodness for Peter and John,
Who both appeared at that very moment
Confirming the body was gone.
I didn't know to be joyous or sad
Till they explained what it meant:
"He said that in three days He'd rise,
He's finally Death's bonds rent!"

I am not sure how that spoke to them,
I know what it said to me.
That short time I looked into his eyes
And gave all, had set me free.
Not that it was me at all,
It was He who lured me in.
It was He who gave my heart the call,
And He who broke my sin.

Many years have passed since that day
Yet I'm as close right now
To Jesus as I was back then
When I close my eyes and bow.
I can feel Him in the very room—
A Peace just permeates all.
My heart begins to burn like fire
When I'm quiet to hear His call.

He is the Risen Lord, indeed,
He's conquered death and sin
And vitally important for me
He's set all aright within.

O' CHRIST, ALL LOVE EMBRACING (Tune, "O' Sacred Head")

How sep'rate, lone and helpless
Devoid of love and tears,
Embrace me in Thy Caress
Dispel my wretched Fears
Hold me against Thy breast, Lord,
To feel Thy Fire of Love
Transcendent in Thy Splendor
All Powerful Lamb and Dove.

In depths my soul Thou searchest
My lifelong Journey's Quest,
And painf'lly Thou yet knowest
Named answers to Thy Rest.
For this same wilderness road
Thou hast before me trod
Thorns, spikes and goring chest goad
Bore Thou for me, O God.

Thou pierce my heart clear through, Lord
With Thy Redeeming Grace.
Spend all my blackest sins, Lord
Might I behold Thy Face.
Pray touch me, hold me, love me,
Walk by my side alway,
Until my Journey's end sees
Heaven's Never Ending Day!

THE TELLY

I'd like to be a telephone
And hear what people say
I would travel miles and miles
And be back in just one day.

Better than books 'n radio
To hear what people do
To catch them all unaware
And hear them fuss 'n stew

To capture intimate secrets
Whispered lifelong dreams
To see an occasional tear or two
Shed over lovers' themes

I'd step inside another's world
Ride their words for awhile
Waiting for the apt reply
Shot in verbose style.

Better than a letter
Or stereo and TV
It even caps my DVD
Phones are just my cup of tea!

I hope I didn't bore you
With my sophistries and all
And if you ever need a friend
Just pick up the phone...and call!

POSTLOGUE

(My own word - a "last" prologue)

Some keys to unlock several poems that are benefited by explanation:

Calculated Cocktails - How many times I attended these "parties" offered by drug representatives. I was a young resident, inexperienced in the upper class settings. Most attendees were more bored than I. Thus, this poem.

That Old Coat - I was a folk singer. Simon and Garfunkel were among my favorites. This poem was a remembrance of their piece "Old Friends." From young, to active, to settling down with other old friends, this Coat tells a story.

Rambling - On a college fraternity weekend in Gatlinburg, TN, I met a sorority poet. We enjoyed sharing our minds for an evening, and kept a written relationship thereafter. We discussed peanut butter and flowers provoking this poem.

Weave - One of my precious memories. My 12 year old daughter came to me one evening and exclaimed, "Daddy! I have to have a poem for class tomorrow! I've never written a poem. Can you teach me?" I asked her questions: What would you like to write about? What about colors? A flag? What are flags used for? And I began to show her how to write a poem.

Looking Back - My one-year old grandson was so delightful at his first birthday. This poem poured forth as I watched him growing up.

Rainfall -Most scribblings are images of real events. This one is from a drive down I-26 in a hearty thunderstorm. And what comes after?

Forty Years - My best friend's 40th birthday brought forth these images.

Anarchy of the Heart - My most difficult poem. This is about my left-brain fighting my right brain. Left-brain is all about schedules, calendars, regulations, while right-brain summons dreams, art, poetry, music, and sometimes procrastination. Try it again.

Memories Become Us - They are often not about "jeans", but "genes".

Bottled Love - Awaking from a morning dream I envisioned a green bottle lying on my dresser. There was no bottle, or dresser, but this poem was born.

Evening of French - One of my favorites, came to me after having a delightful French meal with my young bride-to-be.

Fair Lady - Yes, I loved her so much...I wanted her to know me as who I wished I was, not as who I saw myself.

Golden Girl - So many days of dreams drawn into one poem about my true love. Who is yours?

Heartstrings - I was trying to pull her closer, wanting her to love me more. Pull - or not?

Dreams - They are so real, so captivating, that awakening is too unreal.

Skylight Afternoon - Moments too blissful to pass by unwritten. Truly love engaged.

Beach Getaway - Have you ever watched your love's shadow on the sand as she (or he) runs, exhillarant in the sand, the sun, the crashing waves?

Grass and Green Grass - Such a summer afternoon, balmy, breezy, soft and comfortable with her at my side. Ahhh, the grass...

Beachcomber - I live by the beach. There are few sunny afternoons more mellow than lying on soft sand, arm in arm.

Roses and Gaze - She is gone. My love engaged is lost. Will she return?

My Plea - I see him, my ancestor, Edgar Allen Poe, in this. One of my few longer poems with rhyme and rhythm and dark sadness

Sighs - Life without love, a deep darkness, a dreadful depression, a midnight longing.

Retrospect - Introspect without prospect.

Love Warriors - Two close individuals, jilted, and finding each other now joining into one.

Sixty Years - Memories on my 60th birthday.

September 11th - World events are abruptly shattering. This poem erupted after the News.

Hurricane Hugo - As a doctor I was required to remain during Hugo as my family fled north. I walked the beaches midst tatterings of others' lives.

Lost Gem - My wife and I were watching a friend play in a tennis match. She quietly said, "You must write about the hurricane in New Orleans." I tried arguing, but these lines flooded onto my tennis match program.

College Memories and Exam Sanctuary -College days are indelibly imprinted in our souls.

Life of a Leaf - Written in my second college year. Depressed, lonely, expressed as a falling leaf, and my first poem written.

Fool and Stone Man - My self-vision as a Freshman in an all-male college. Those were the days.

Breakin' Out - Written while on a meditation journey, this is a Lenten Meditation worthy of slow and thoughtful reading.

O Christ - A poem that formed as I listened to the tune of "O Sacred Head Now Wounded," which I would like to present to a hymnal official for review and consideration.

The Telly - My father would often speak to us with an English accent. The "telly", when I was a child, referred to a telephone, not the television of today. Read and laugh a bit.

I am glad you made it this far. So have I! If you enjoyed your experience, try it again. Sometime.

It would be great to have criticism, positive (Yes!), and negative (we all have to learn, don't we?). My email address is:

johnkul007@gmail.com when your fingers are light.

I have many more poems and have read them on CD's. Listening may be easier than reading them. See the list below. A pleasant day to you!

Jon Jacobs

HOW TO ORDER

PHOTOCOPY this page and mail or fax as below.

LIFESCAPES - HARDBACK BOOK $25.95

LIFESCAPES - PAPER BACK BOOK $11.95

LIFESCAPES - AUDIO - MUSINGS $ 9.95

LIFESCAPES - AUDIO - LOVE SOUGHT $ 9.95

LIFESCAPES - AUDIO - LOVE ENGAGED $ 9.95

LIFESCAPES - AUDIO - LOVE LOST $ 9.95

LIFESCAPES - AUDIO - IDIOSYNCRASIES $ 9.95

LIFESCAPES - AUDIO - VARIOUS POEMS $ 9.95

EMAIL: johnkul007@gmail.com

FAX: 843-572-9165 (Include face sheet with address and Visa or Master Card number)

MAIL: Jon R Jacobs Books, 233 Marsh Oaks Dr, Charleston, SC 29407

Please include payment in Money Order, Check, Visa or Master Card info, return address!

www.ingramcontent.com/pod-product-compliance
Lightning Source LLC
Chambersburg PA
CBHW071017040426
42443CB00007B/813